7 Trades to a Million

For anybody with a small account and a big dream

7 Trades to a Million

Jack Winthrop

Published by Amazon

Chapter 1:
The Introduction

On December 14th, 2019 Tesla was trading at $430 per share after already being up 50% on the year. A member of an online investment forum with the username Ambudriver03, an ambulance driver and Tesla fan invested $14 into Tesla calls expiring two months later. When he sold that call just 28 days after he bought it, he had turned $14 into $14,124 for over a 100,000% gain.

A few months later, another user on the same thread posted a 200,000% gain on Tesla options, turning a $436 investment into $928,700 over the span of 8 months. Even though the stock only went up a few hundred percent, if you can use the same options strategies that hedge funds do, you can create insane returns.

There were seemingly millions of people who were sure Tesla would skyrocket during that time, however, investors in common stock did not even see their money double. Investors in derivatives like the call option described above could create returns that most in the investing community would tell you are impossible. The mission of this book is to prove that lottery winning returns in the stock market are possible for anybody and to teach you how to turn any investing budget into a fortune.

The example of our ambulance driver shows the power of derivatives trading and how we can use it to create massive returns. However, we do not need a 100,000% gain to turn $5 of pocket change into a million. We just need 7 trades of a much more manageable 600% as shown below. If we take $5 and earn 600% 7 times we get:

$5→ $30→ $180→ $1,080→ $6,480→ $38,880→ $233,280→ $1,399,680

This is called compounding interest and Albert Einstein called it "the 8th wonder of the world". Using the derivatives strategies in this book, anybody can achieve a 600% trade. In fact, the odds of hitting 7 600% trades in a row are far *far* greater than playing the lottery yet the lottery has 90 million annual players in the US and the strategies in this book are largely unknown.

Due to asymmetric risk, derivatives trading is also a much better proposition than sports betting. Asymmetric risk is simply the idea that one side of an equation has a different level of risk than the other. When trading options you are entering into a situation of extreme asymmetric risk where you can win far more than you can lose. When you are betting on a point spread in sports, you can only win as much as you risk.

The key difference between playing the lottery or betting on sports compared to playing the stock market is that the lottery commission and the bookmakers rigged the game for you to lose while the stock market is rigged for you to win. There are many facets of life in the United States that are based on the stock market going up and that is why there are so many opportunities for a 600%+ trade. Even if you were just paying attention to what you ate for breakfast.

For example, during the beginning of the COVID-19 outbreak in the United States it did not take a financial genius to see that people were stocking up on canned and pantry goods. Grocery stores were packed and they could not keep the many of the popular pantry products on the shelves. It got to a point where government officials were pleading with people not to buy more than they needed.

At this time from March 25th to April 3rd, Campbell's Soup stock went up 20%. A move like this is enough to conservatively create a return in the 1,000% range using the correct options plays. Even if you missed this, their competitor General Mills, who own Progresso soup and many leading cereal brands were set to report earnings after Campbell's. If you had purchased a short term call option on General Mills after Campbells already reported positive earnings outlook you would have still easily cleared the 600% threshold. This is after Campbell's had already made its move.

Paying attention to the world we live in is the key to finding our 6x opportunities. Once we find these opportunities, we need to use the derivatives strategies we will talk about later and timing to capitalize on them.

Throughout this book, we will directly address the financial industry and how the Bell Curve distribution shows that our "genius" investors are not quite geniuses. We talk about why you would actually lose money by not investing and go through everything you need to know about the investing industry and stocks to make your first trade. We will then teach you about options, triple leveraged ETFs and end with how to construct a winning portfolio.

The goal of this book is to give you all the information you need as fast as possible without wasting time on the minutiae of investing. All you have to do to get rich in the stock market is understand the basic principles in this book and pay attention to your surroundings.

Chapter 2:
The Bell Curve

In the world of investing, we assume that we are playing a game of skill instead of luck. Any analysis of the current investment climate would show that this is not completely the case. To beat the investing world, we have to be able to harness luck and take calculated chances in the same way that the top hedge funds do.

Luck is the single biggest factor in all our lives. Where you were born, who your parents are, your biological make-up, and thus the opportunities you started life with are all based on luck and play a huge factor in your life. Throughout your life things that are completely outside of your control play a huge role even though we typically explain them away. In the investing world, luck is an important element and something that we must embrace.

Imagine that everybody in the world flipped a coin 100 times. The average of over 7 billion trials would be 50 heads and 50 tails. In a graph of all 7 billion trials most of the people would be bunched together with 45 to 55 of their flips being heads and the opposite being tails. Being outside of that range would be much more rare. In a sample size as large as the amount of people in the world there are going to be some outliers. There will be some very extreme cases where people get far more heads or tails than the average. We can see how this graphed distribution would look by using the next chart called a "Bell Curve".

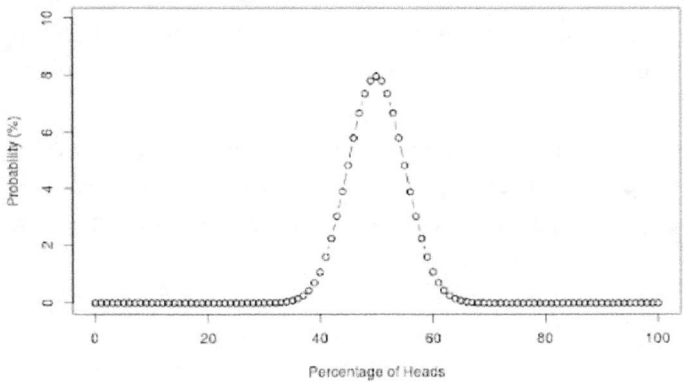

This Bell Curve is a very important tool for understanding variability in statistics and it presents itself everywhere in nature. In the example of coin flipping there is no skill involved but the natural distribution of random probabilities will create a perfect bell curve. The main indication that this is luck and not skill is that in a second trial we would see no correlation between the number of heads one person flipped in the first trial and the number of heads the same person flipped in the second trial.

If somebody were able to cheat the game with a weighted coin that landed on heads more often, they would be consistently on the far-right side of the bell curve and prove that they are not just getting lucky since they would have consistent results. A person who can get more heads every time with a weighted coin is outside the bounds of luck because they are cheating. Everybody else would still fluctuate wildly from trial to trial with no correlation to their previous spot on the bell curve since flipping a coin is a game of pure luck.

Some examples of perfect bell curves that are widely accepted as factors outside of our control include: height (pictured below), IQ, and running speed.

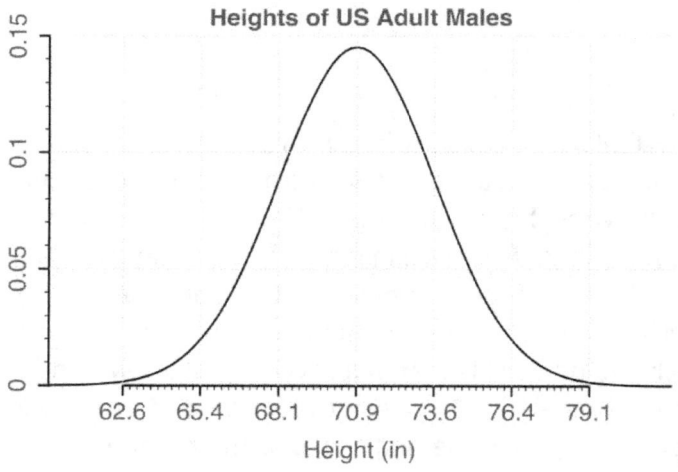

In the professional investing world, hedge funds aim to achieve the highest possible returns. Hedge funds are investment companies usually based in New York or Connecticut that take on billions of dollars from institutional investors and play the stock market. The institutional investors are organizations that operate with a large cash float such as: college endowments, pension funds, very wealthy families, and other large money managers. More on that later. These hedge funds, named because they are a hedge against other investment strategies, take risks in the stock market to achieve returns for their investors.

The two sides to the hedge fund industry are raising money and investing money. Raising money is getting institutional investors to give you their money to invest for them. This consists of pitch meetings and is a process only run by the top one or two people in the hedge fund. If a fund has $1 billion to invest, they probably raised $50 million each from 20 different institutional investors. The hedge fund then invests this money with the promise to give the institutional investors back more money at the end of a 5-to-10-year period. The hedge fund makes money by taking a percentage of the money they gained from investing before giving it all back.

Most hedge funds get paid based on a "2 and 20" structure that states they can keep 2% of the money they initially raised every year and 20% of the returns they make from investing it. For example, if a hedge fund raises $1 billion dollars and grows it to $1.5 billion at the end of a 5-year period; they receive $20 million each year as the 2% of the original $1 billion and $100 million at the end since it is 20% of the $500 million extra that they made. The rest of the money goes back to the investors. Over this 5-year period the hedge fund would make $200 million dollars.

A $1 billion sized hedge fund is not very big in the investing world and would usually consist of about 5 to 10 people choosing the investments and another 5 to 10 people doing administrative work. Of the $200 million they made from investing during this 5-year period, the investment team receives a majority of the earnings. On the investment team the lion's share would be made by the top one or two guys at the hedge fund.

Hedge funds are judged based on IRR which stands for internal rate of return and basically means the percent they grow the fund each year. In the example above, the IRR is about 8.4% since they grew the fund an average of 8.4% each year to get from $1 billion to $1.5 billion in 5 years.

8.4% does not sound so bad on its own but hedge funds and all investors in the stock market are judged against the S&P 500. The S&P 500 is a group of stocks selected by the publication Standard & Poors that are meant to represent all sectors of the market.

The sectors include:

Communication Services: Social Media, Regular Media, and Telephone Carriers

Consumer Discretionary: Retailers, Automobiles, Hotels, and Restaurants

Consumer Staples: Food, Beverages, Hygiene, and Personal Products

Energy: Oil and Gas

Financials: Banks, Insurance Companies, Consumer Lenders, and Investment Firms

Health Care: Pharmaceuticals, Hospitals, Biotechnology, and Equipment Providers

Industrials: Manufacturers, Airlines, Defense, Railroads, and Machinery

Materials: Chemicals, Metals, Mining, Paper, and Lumber

Real Estate: Real Estate Investment Trusts and Owners of Real Estate

Technology: Hardware, Software, IT, and Semiconductor

Utilities.: Electric, Water, and Renewable Energy

The stocks in the S&P 500 are some of the most consistent companies on the market while underperformers are dropped from the index. To be considered for the S&P 500, a company must hit certain value and profit thresholds.

When people talk about the market as a whole, they are usually describing the performance of the S&P 500 or similar groups of stocks such as the Dow Jones Index. When people say, "the market is up", they are referring to these indexes.

Below is a chart of the S&P 500 over the last 30 years. As you can see, the market generally goes up, in fact the average year over year performance of the S&P 500 is approximately 10%. This means that all the stocks in the S&P 500 index go up on average 10% per year since 1926 when the index was started.

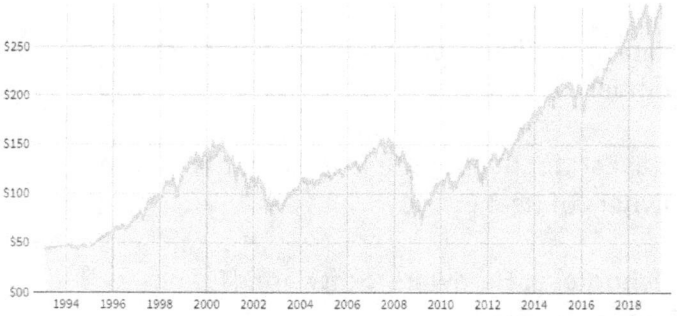

If everyone from the coin flipping experiment picked any handful of stocks from this index at random the middle of the global bell curve would be a 10% annual gain. This means that any random selection of stocks is already expected to achieve 10% returns no matter how they are picked. This is famously described by Princeton University professor Burton Malkiel who wrote: "A blindfolded monkey throwing darts at a newspaper's financial pages could select a portfolio that would do just as well as one carefully selected by experts." While 10% is the center of the bell curve for any random selection of stocks, done by either monkeys or financial experts, some randomly chosen portfolios would certainly be outliers just like in our coin flipping example. It would be expected that one of our monkeys picking stocks would be able to achieve returns well above the market and even into the 100% return range if they were lucky enough to throw darts at stocks that doubled during that year.

Malkiel later proved his hypothesis correct by having a group of monkeys pick stocks by throwing darts at a large wall of tickers. While the monkeys were not blindfolded, many of them did beat the market average with their portfolios.

In this case our hypothetical hedge fund from earlier would have done worse than the average monkey picking stocks since they only achieved an IRR of 8.4% per year. The difference is that the hedge fund earned $200 million over 5 years even though they performed worse than you would expect monkeys to.

But as we said earlier, just because something is a bell curve does not mean that it is based on luck. In the coin flipping example, if somebody used a weighted coin, they would no longer be subject to luck and could consistently land in the far right of the bell curve. Being able to consistently land in the same spot of the bell curve shows that there is a reason other than luck that makes a data point an outlier. Batting averages in baseball present a good example of this.

Many people argue that hitting a baseball is the hardest thing to do in any sport. Major League hitters are weeded out from a pool of millions of little leaguers, high schoolers, college players, and minor league players as the best in the world at hitting a baseball. Even among the best hitters in the world the chart of MLB averages makes a bell curve as shown in the next chart.

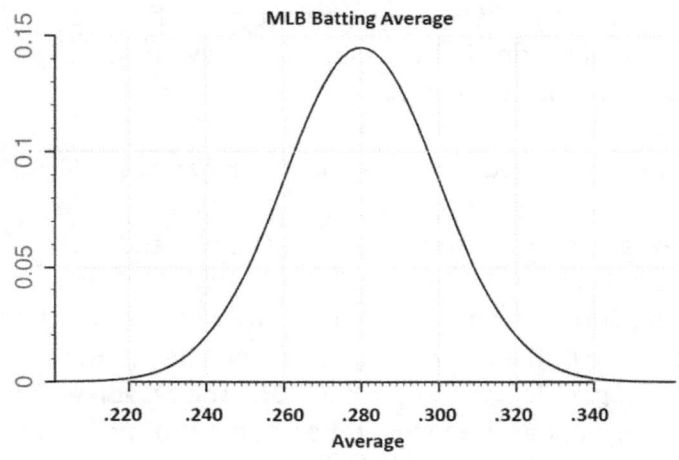

Beyond the seemingly obvious skill it takes to hit a baseball in the major leagues, the bell curve of hitters proves that baseball is based on skill and not luck. The best hitters are able to consistently land on the far-right side of the bell curve year after year over 20-year careers. Ty Cobb batted .366 over his entire career and never had a season below .320 after officially breaking into the big leagues. This is 21 straight years of being on the very far right of the bell curve and this proves that he was there through skill and not luck. If you look at any hitter from the charted distribution, you would find that they would land in a similar place year over year because the MLB bell curve is based on skill and not luck. Conversely, in a coin flipping bell curve there is no correlation between trials. People who had more heads in one trial would not have a better chance to get more heads in the next trial. Baseball players who bat in the .300s one year have a much higher chance of batting in the .300s the next year since baseball is based on skill.

The standardized testing world embraces the bell curve and even scores candidates based on where they land on the curve. Tests like the SAT and ACT give a raw score and a percentile score. If you score in the 80th percentile that means that you are on the right side of the bell curve having done better than 80% of people and worse than 20%. The reason we rely on standardized tests is because it is proven that test taking is based on skill and fluctuations for the same candidate from test to test are minimal. The test would be useless if a candidate that scored in the 80th percentile could regularly score in the 20th percentile if they took the test again.

When we look at the distribution of hedge funds on the bell curve from decade to decade, we find that the top performers are not able to stay on the right side of the curve. There is almost no correlation between being in the top performers in one decade and being there the next. Even Warren Buffett, who is widely viewed as the greatest investor of all time, underperformed compared to the S&P 500s returns in the 2010s. This does not just put him outside of the top percentile of investors, but his performance puts him below the average you would expect from a group of blindfolded monkeys throwing darts. Warren Buffet is still widely praised and regularly makes appearances at investing conferences to give advice despite below average performance for over a decade. Ty Cobb, who is widely viewed as the greatest hitter for average of all time, never had a season outside of the top 5%, Buffet has had a decade outside the top 50%. Since Buffet was not able to stay on the right side of the bell curve it is possible that his success in the 80s and 90s was due to luck. In the same way, we would expect somebody to flip 90 heads out of 100 tries if everyone in the world was flipping coins.

The goal of this section is not to prove that investing is purely luck but simply to show that many top hedge fund managers and investors are largely where they are because of luck and anybody should be able to use the same strategies they do to invest in the stock market. By using their strategies and acknowledging that luck is a huge factor, we can put ourselves in the same positions to succeed that they do. Since our goal is to make money instead of proving we are sophisticated investors, we can beat hedge funds using their same strategies.

For example, Michael Burry is a famous hedge fund manager portrayed in "The Big Short". He famously shorted the market before the 2008 financial crisis and made his investors rich. Before the market dropped, Burry received many requests from investors to pull out their money which almost put Burry out of business before he could see the returns of his short position. While Burry ended up being right, other hedge fund managers were all proven wrong. These hedge fund managers that were proven wrong were still able to raise additional funds in the future. In the hedge fund industry, it is a bigger risk to go against the grain than to follow the pack. Hedge funds are mainly paid as a function of how much money they raise from institutional investors, not how much money they make from investing it.

The entire investment industry is based on proving that investing is not luck since billions of dollars can be raised by those with "skill". Remember how our hypothetical hedge fund earned $200 million dollars in 5 years by doing worse than we would expect monkeys to do? They are viewed as sophisticated investors. They write long white papers on industry trends, hire smart people from Ivy League Schools, and some of them even have proprietary algorithms that are "proven" to beat the market. However, the way they make money is hardly through picking the right stocks since in our example they picked below average stocks and still made $200 million with their 2 and 20 payment structure. The most important factor for a hedge fund to make money is to raise money by convincing their investors that they are picking stocks with skill and not luck.

This understanding of how hedge funds make money shows that they are playing a different game than the average investor. Hedge funds seek to create good enough returns to continue to raise money since they get paid based on how much money they raise. Individual investors get paid based on how much money they can make through investing in the market itself.

The success of the investment industry is based on proving that professional investors are sophisticated, and we are not, otherwise why would we give them our money to invest? This is why the fundamentals of investing are not widely known and most people do not invest for themselves even though they absolutely should.

Most people in the investment industry will tell you to stay away from options, triple leveraged ETFs, and volatile stocks. Recently, options trading surpassed the volume of regular stocks, yet it is still considered irresponsible to trade them. In the later chapters we will explain exactly how anybody can use options and other unknown strategies to make a fortune in the stock market.

Since we are trying to make money instead of trying to prove we are sophisticated investors, we already have a leg up on Wall Street. Since we do not have to justify our decisions to the broader investment community, we can embrace that luck is a factor in investing. We can use the high-risk strategies that are reserved for hedge funds only and we can pursue ridiculous returns that they want you to believe are impossible.

Chapter 2:
Scared Money Don't Make Money

Our fear of loss is greater than our desire for gain. This is called loss aversion and it is something we all understand even if we don't acknowledge it. The basic premise of loss aversion is that we are unable to fairly evaluate risk because humans evolved to avoid losses. A caveman has no reason to risk anything of necessity to make gains beyond what he needs for survival. Avoiding losses at the expense of gains is hardwired into our subconscious mind and hard to avoid. Unfortunately, our instincts are designed to keep us alive, not make us rich, as our gut reactions are driven by our subconscious mind.

Loss aversion is one of the main cognitive biases exploited by advertising because people are driven by fear. Advertising campaigns try to invent scarcity with "limited time" sales and hope to convince people to act now with the fear of missing their chance. Loss aversion marketing is also common in the medical field where the losses can more deeply affect our subconscious fear of death.

A Harvard study aiming to prove how fear affects motivation used two different brochures to test a patient's reactions on cancer prevention. One of the brochures emphasized the gains of performing self-exams, while the other brochure emphasized the losses of not performing self-exams. The study found that the negatively framed brochures did around 400% better than the positively framed ones. In the medical field, life or death thinking might make more sense, but this frame of mind carries over into finance as well. We must be aware of our tendency to ignore possible gains and only focus on losses, especially when it comes to money.

A study done by David Kahneman and his associate Amos Tversky, first proved loss aversion in 1979 by examining how people risk money. They tested and proved their theory by exploring people's tolerance for risk vs reward. A newer study that recreates Tversky and Kahneman's work begins with three groups of randomly assorted participants. The first group was given $5 and was told that they could either keep it or risk it on a coin flip for the chance to win $15. This is an example of asymmetrically weighted probabilities, rationally thinking, you should take a 50% chance to triple your money. A computer programmed to maximize its amount of money would accept this risk at every probability down to a 33.3%. This is the level where the risk is equal to the reward of tripling your money. With a coin flip you get a 50% chance, so it is a positive expected value proposition, meaning that taking a 50% risk to triple your money is expected to earn you more money. Unsurprisingly, most people agreed, 84% of people took the risk and flipped the coin for the chance to walk away with $15. When they raised the amount of money given to you to $50 and the possible winnings of the coin flip to $150 the number of people willing to take the same exact risk went down to 57%. When the researchers raised the numbers to $500 and $1,500 only 12% of people were willing to take the same mathematically favorable risk. While the study did not go further, if they raised the winnings to $3,000 off the same $500 risk it would not have much of an effect on the people willing to take the risk and flip the coin. This study proves that while we can determine which calculated risks to take, it is more difficult to do so when the fear of losing is involved. Losing $5 does not trigger our fear of loss as much as $500 does so people were less willing to take the same risk. To make money in the stock market we must be willing to risk more than we can stomach.

There are many ways to invest that require the minimum amount of risk and some with no risk at all. To go from a small account to $1 million, we need to embrace risk and understand that in many cases our instinctual reaction is to avoid risks. We will look for calculated risks and ones where the odds are greatly in our favor. In the example of the $500 vs $3,000 you can use percentages to evaluate either option. In the $500 option you have a 100% chance of walking away with $500 so your expected value is $500. Expected value is a way for us to calculate the value of taking a risk by evaluating the probability and return of all outcomes. In the $3,000 option you have a 50% chance of walking away with $0 and a 50% chance of walking away with $3,000. This means that the expected value is $1,500, 3x greater than option one (the expected value for a $1,500 option would be $750). In this scenario, it makes sense to take the calculated risk because your expected value is higher. Even if you lose, taking the risk was still the correct decision.

While in the stock market, we generally want to avoid all or nothing risks; it is essential that we are comfortable with some level of risk. In fact, not investing at all is a risk itself due to inflation and the time value of money or net present value.

Prices always get higher because of inflation: you may have noticed that five-dollar footlongs are no longer on the market and that in the 1920's, a bottle of Coke only cost five cents. The United States Federal Reserve has mandated an approximately 2% inflation rate for the foreseeable future. The Federal Reserve controls inflation through a few methods but mainly through interest rates and money supply. Inflation is measured using the Consumer Price Index (CPI) which tells us how much the same basket of goods and services would cost in a different time. As the price of goods and services goes up over time, the value of the dollar goes down. A 2% inflation rate means losing 2% of your money every year because the value of what you can buy with it goes down 2%. This means that if you are not investing to earn at least 2% of your money each year, then you are accepting a loss each year as your money becomes less valuable.

Inflation is one of the main reasons why people use gold and other precious metals as a means to store money. While gold is not a perfect hedge against inflation, it is certainly meaningful that today a one-ounce gold coin costs about $2,000. Which is enough to stay 5 nights at a standard room in the Plaza Hotel in New York for $200 per night. If you had that same ounce of gold in 1920 it would be worth $250 and back then a room at the Plaza costs exactly $50 a night. While the dollar value of gold has changed, one ounce of gold has always gotten you five nights at the Plaza Hotel. Gold has relatively kept its value over the last 100 years since you could get the same exact product with the same amount of gold in 1920. The dollar on the other hand has lost its value and will continue to.

Even more powerful than inflation is the net present value of money (NPV). The NPV of money takes into account the opportunity cost of not investing and reflects how smart investors think about their money. The basic premise of NPV is that money today is worth more than money tomorrow because you can grow the money you have today to be worth more tomorrow. For example, if you can grow your money at 10% per year and you have the choice between getting $100,000 today or $105,000 next year, you should take the $100,000 today. $100,000 today is worth more than $105,000 next year because you can invest $100,000 today to turn into $110,000 next year since you can grow it at 10%.

Inflation is also a factor here but the opportunity cost of not growing your money is the largest reason why money today is worth more than money tomorrow.

I went to college with a lot of South Korean students who were taught NPV from a young age. In South Korea, the entire real estate system hinges on the idea of NPV. When you rent an apartment in South Korea you have two payment options: Jeon-se and Wol-se. We will label these options as Option A and Option B.

In Option A, you have the opportunity to pay a deposit worth 50-80% of the entire apartment's value but you pay no rent over the course of your lease and you get the entire deposit back at the end.

In Option B you pay a small upfront deposit like the American system and you pay monthly rent throughout your lease. In Option B you still get your small deposit back, but you do not get the monthly rent back.

Almost all Americans will tell you to take Option A because you do not lose any money and you get everything back in the end, however, in Korea this is correctly viewed as a suckers bet. Let's break down the options using numbers to see why.

Assuming the apartment is worth $200k here is how both options would break down.

Option A:
- Deposit $150k (75% of the apartment's value)
- No monthly rent
- Get back $150k deposit after two years

You start with $150k and at the end of two years you still have $150k

Option B
- Deposit $10k (5% of apartments value)
- Monthly rent of $1k
- Get back $10k deposit after two years

You start with $150k and at the end of two years you paid $24k of rent so you have $126k.

Since over the course of the lease you paid 24 months' rent in Option B you are down by $24k. However, since your deposit was only $10k you still had $140k left over to invest at the start of your lease. Let's say you put that $140k in the S&P 500 index fund that goes up 10% per year. Now at the end of your first year you made $14k from your investment and only spent $12k on rent. You can take that additional $2k and add it to your investment and invest $142k in the second year. Now at the end of your second year of 10% returns you made $14,200 on your investment and spent only $12k on rent. You also get your $10,000 deposit back plus the $144,200 you have from investing. At the end of Option B's two-year period, you have $154,200 compared to the $150k you would get back from Option A.

While a $4,200 difference seems marginal, in this case we were using the conservative 10% returns. Using 20% returns, the difference would be $35,200 and using the returns from the S&P in 2019 of 31% the difference would be $79,000. You would end the lease with $219,000 from investing even though you were paying $1,000 per month rent. As you can see if you are able to use the most basic market tracking instruments you can invest and make more money. Therefore, refusing to invest hurts your savings on a net present value and an inflation basis.

In the example above, you can see that when we invested $140k and earned 10% on it we then had more money to earn 10% on the next year. This is called compounding interest and Albert Einstein famously said that "Compounding interest is the 8th wonder of the world. He who understands it, earns it; he who doesn't pays it". It is a shame that we do not teach elementary students about compounding interest as understanding it is one of the largest factors in growing wealth. I can assure you that if you ask somebody scared to invest: "how many years does it take to double your money if you earn 10% every year?" they will say 10 years. Using the example from above we can see that is not true.

Let's say you live with your parents instead of paying rent and take the same $150,000 from above and invest it in a market tracking index that grows 10% per year.

Year 0: $150,000
Year 1: $165,000
Year 2: $181,500
Year 3: $199,650
Year 4: $219,615
Year 5: $242,576
Year 6: $265,734
Year 7: $293,516
Year 7, month 2: $300,000

It takes 7 years and 2 months to double your money at 10% per year. If you kept your money in for another 7 years you would have quadrupled your money in 14 years. However, the goal of this book is to show you how you can achieve much faster returns and achieve these gains in 14 months instead of 14 years.

The Native Americans famously sold the island of Manhattan for $24 in 1626. While this is usually considered an unfair deal, we can see how this may have been a good proposition through compounding interest if managed correctly. If the Native Americans had taken that $24 and invested it in a market tracking index returning 10% per year over the next 400 years, they would have over $8 Trillion today.

They would have enough to buy back Manhattan after it was already redeveloped and modernized.

Many people would be surprised to know that Warren Buffet has averaged only 20% annual returns over the course of his investing career. Starting when he was 14 years old with only a few thousand he reached a million when he turned 30 and did not reach a billion dollars until he was 56. At 90 years old, he has about $80 billion dollars which he has pledged to give all away to charity.

While Warren Buffet has done a lot for humanity by making such a large charitable contribution, his lifestyle begs the question: Would you rather be Warren Buffet or Jimmy Buffet?

Warren Buffet notoriously lived in his same Omaha house his entire life and eats either a Big Mac or a single McDonald's cheeseburger for lunch depending on if the market is up or down. He is estimated to have spent almost none of his wealth in his life and has invested everything he had in the stock market. After waiting 90 years he eventually gave the entire fortune away.

Jimmy Buffet is one of the most famous musicians of the 20th century and invented the "Caribbean rock n' roll" genre. He has multiple large mansions including one in Palm Beach and one on a Caribbean Island where he spends most of his time. He is the owner of

Margaritaville one of the nation's most well-known restaurant chains and the writer of the hit song "Cheeseburger in Paradise". Presumably, Jimmy Buffet's cheeseburgers are higher quality than McDonalds and are enjoyed outside of Omaha, Nebraska. They likely do not fluctuate in size based on how the market is doing that day.

While Warren Buffet is an example of the power of compounding interest, he is not the model we should follow for our entire account. Warren is famously risk averse; he does not invest in any companies before they prove to be profitable. This is part of the reason that he has done worse than the indexes over the last decade. "The Wizard of Omaha" as he is known, has missed out on almost all of tech because he refused to invest in companies that were not yet profitable. Even if you would rather be Warren than Jimmy, we should still avoid making the same mistake.

While a section of our investment portfolio will be relatively safe, we will need to be comfortable taking big risks to get the big returns we want. Sometimes this will mean ignoring our instincts and trusting our strategy instead of our gut.

Chapter 3:
Secrets of the 1%

Why don't we teach our children how to invest their money? High school kids are forced to take trigonometry, gym, interpretive dance, and woodworking but we never teach them how to passively invest in the stock market. Unfamiliarity with the stock market leads to a great fear of investing as half of Americans do not own any stocks at all. The stock market is the greatest tool for wealth generation in the history of mankind and yet it is completely overlooked and brushed over by the American schooling system.

The large gaps in knowledge between investing professionals and regular people help the finance industry generate fees. As we mentioned in Chapter 1, the two primary ways that investing institutions get paid are by taking a cut of the money they raise to invest and taking a cut of the profits that they generate through investing. To continue to raise money and generate fees, it is in the best interest of professional investors to tell the masses that it is too risky to invest for themselves. That is why the investment industry tells us not to invest for ourselves.

Some of the highest paying professions in America include doctors, surgeons, engineers, computer programmers, and investing professionals. Only one of these professions can be outperformed by a monkey with darts. A monkey could not do any profession better than the average human except for investing. This begs the question of why hedge fund managers are paid so much, and the answer is that their job consists more of convincing people they can beat the market than actually beating the market. A monkey likely could not do the first part. In this chapter we will unveil the curtain covering the investment industry and talk about how it currently works.

Most of the money in the American financial system belongs to the large institutional investors. These include college endowments, pension funds, insurance companies or any institution with a large cash float that must invest the money due to inflation and opportunity costs from NPV. A cash float is a large sum of money that is generated by an organization's regular operations and must be invested. Cash floats must be invested because the companies are still on the hook for the money in some way. An insurance company cannot just pay themselves all the insurance premiums because they are mandated to keep a certain amount of cash on hand to pay off claims. The same can be said for commercial lenders and credit card companies. Insurance companies take all of the money we pay them monthly into a cash float and invest it to grow the money while they pay out their claims. It is interesting to note that Warren Buffet's Berkshire Hathaway owns Geico, General Re (the largest reinsurance company in America), and American Express; all companies with large cash floats that must be reinvested. The difference in strategy between institutional investors and individual investors is large because institutions could not afford a down year where they lost money. For example, if a pension fund lost 5% of its fund, that could seriously jeopardize the retirement of its beneficiaries in that year. Whereas an individual can afford to lose 5% in the market in a given year because they know that it will be made back over time as the 100+ year history of the stock market holds an average of 8.4% annual gains with only a few down years.

Institutional investors target 2% to 4% gains and invest in a lot of instruments such as bonds and commodities that do not make sense for our portfolio. Let's take a look at Harvard's endowment to see how they invest.

Next is a chart of how Harvard's $41 billion endowment is invested with the percentage they have in each asset allocation.

Harvard Endowment	
Asset	**%**
Domestic Equity	11%
Foreign Equity	11%
Emerging Market Equity	11%
Private Equity	18%
Total Equity	**51%**
Natural Resources	11%
Real Estate	12%
Total Real Assets	**23%**
Fixed Income	**10%**

Of the approximately $41 billion portfolio, 11% is going to domestic equity investments. Of this 11%, most of it will go to investment managers and very safe equity investments, only a small portion will go to hedge funds that try to achieve the high returns we aim for in this book. Since hedge funds are such a small portion of the overall portfolio, Harvard encourages them to take risks to maximize returns because if they lose money it will hardly affect the larger endowment.

Some hedge funds try to take risks in the market to maximize potential gains. They use stocks, options, and sometimes even high yield loans to make as much money as possible with a large amount of risk. Other hedge funds are used as hedges against the overall market such as funds that only short stocks called "short only funds". As you can imagine, it is much more difficult to make money betting on which stocks will go down; but in the larger institutional portfolio, it is good to have a short only fund that will drastically rise if the market has a down year to offset the majority long focused funds.

The most common forms of hedge funds include Long / Short, Quantitative, Market Neutral, Activist, Merger Arbitrage, and Credit. Today, many hedge funds use a mix of these strategies, but these are the most popular strategies in hedge fund investing. Each strategy is described below:

Long/Short hedge funds attempt to beat the market through buying or shorting relatively speculative positions. These are the hedge funds we usually hear about on TV. They are called long / short hedge funds because they are trying to buy or "go long" on stocks they think will go up and "go short" on companies they think will go down.

Quantitative funds write computer algorithms to trade stocks automatically based on data analytics. In a given day, most of the stocks traded on Wall Street are by quantitative funds as they sometimes buy large quantities to sell only moments later based on their algorithms. Many hedge funds employ some form of quant strategies, but we will focus on the fundamental reasons that make a stock more valuable instead of patterns and data analytics.

Market Neutral hedge funds attempt to put together a portfolio that goes up no matter how the market performs, they are expected to have smaller returns than Long/Short hedge funds. Conversely, most hedge funds perform better in years where the market goes up. Market neutral funds are used as a hedge against the overall market and are allowed to produce lower returns as long as they can show that their portfolio is market neutral.

Activist hedge funds seek to purchase a large position in a single company to affect the management and try to improve how the company operates. Usually, the current management is not welcoming to activist funds because this means the fund thinks the management has underperformed. In recent years, AT&T has relatively underperformed the market and made a few large mistakes. Most notably, the purchase of DirectTV in 2015 at the absolute peak of the traditional television market. Since then, the investment has bled subscribers as cord cutting due to Netflix and other alternatives' rise in popularity. This is when Elliot Management, an activist hedge fund, bought a $10 billion stake in AT&T and demanded some changes that could turn the ship around. Since they have such a large stake, it is in the best interest of AT&T to listen to them. If AT&T ignored their advice, Elliot Management could try to get other investors on their side and oust the management team. Activist funds are the most direct example of third-party equity investors affecting a company's management. Usually, investors indirectly affect a company's management because the stock price acts as a gauge for how well the business is doing and collectively as investors, we determine the stock price.

Merger Arbitrage funds try to make money from company mergers and acquisitions. There are a few ways to do this. Public company acquisitions are almost always at a premium of their stock price, meaning that the company is purchased at a stock price higher than the current trading price. If you own a stock that is trading at $5 per share and the company purchased for $10 per share, you doubled your money. After an acquisition is announced the stock usually trades up to or just below the acquisition price because there is a chance that the deal falls through. In this case the stock would trade to something like $9.70 and then up to $10 as the deal gets closer and closer to being finalized. Merger Arbitrage funds attempt to make money on this difference by doing analysis on the likelihood of a deal going through. They also try to figure out which companies will be merged or acquired and buy them before the deals are announced.

Credit funds are different as they do not invest in companies' stock, instead they lend money to distressed companies at very high rates since these companies cannot get the money from anywhere else. Credit funds usually target companies with large risk factors or on the verge of bankruptcy. The credit funds are betting that the company survives and pays back the loan plus a very high interest rate.

Today, many hedge funds use a multitude of the strategies mentioned above and they are all important to know as we follow the stock market. The strategy that we will use most closely resembles a long / short hedge fund. Many investing professionals would tell you that this is too risky and that long / short hedge funds only exist for institutional investors to give a small portion of their money to. This does not hold up because while regular people are not legally allowed to invest in hedge funds, the people who manage them can and in many cases hedge fund managers have much of their own wealth tied up in their funds. If investing like a hedge fund was truly too risky then our professional investment managers would not have such a high percentage of their wealth invested in their own funds.

The next part of Harvard's equity investments will go to investment managers. Investment managers are different from hedge funds because their investors do not want them to take as much risk. Investment managers invest in stable companies and use a mixture of bonds as well. Investment managers can use a small portion of their funds on speculative growth stocks similar to how Harvard can use a small portion of their funds on investing in hedge funds. The investment management industry takes money from institutional investors and regular people who want somebody else to invest their money. They target 5% to 15% returns and include household names like Charles Schwab, Fidelity, BlackRock, PIMCO, and Merrill Lynch.

Bernie Madoff famously ran one of the most successful investment management businesses that turned out to be a Ponzi scheme. Instead of investing the money, Madoff just kept it all in a large fund and told people it was going up about 10% per year. This worked for a very long time until the financial crisis when enough people asked for their money back and he could not pay them back since the money was not actually growing at all. The people who asked for their money back first did receive the fake amount of 10% growth per year plus their investment.

The interesting thing about Madoff is that he was viewed as one of the most successful investment managers and he was generating 11.2% growth. This would put you out of business as a hedge fund manager for poor performance since hedge funds are expected to return 30% or higher annually. The popularity of the investment management industry shows how averse most people are to risk and how much money is left on the table, most people are happy to earn only 5% per year while there are proven strategies to earn much more. People were lining up to pay Bernie Madoff to manage their money because he averaged an 11.2% return year over year. This is barely better than an index fund and the worst part is they ended up losing all their money anyway by attempting to avoid risks.

Investment managers typically take 1% of their entire pool of money each year as a payment to generate market returns. While most people advocate for this strategy you can simply invest in a passive S&P index and match any investment manager's typical returns without paying 1% of your total investment each year.

After domestic equities comes foreign and emerging market equities, these are treated the same as domestic equities above, but they are either in foreign or emerging markets.

The next big chunk of Harvard's endowment goes to Private Equity companies. It is important to know what these are since you will hear about them often in the stock market. While Private Equity companies do not usually own publicly traded companies, they very often acquire public companies at a premium to their share price and take them private. They can also take a private company they already own public through an IPO, if the company is too large for other private market buyers.

Private equity companies use leveraged buyouts (LBOs) to buy private or public companies. This means that they borrow money to buy a company and then pay off the debt with the cash from the company to later sell that company. For example, imagine you have a company that costs $10 billion and it generates $500 million per year. You project that in 5 years the company will be worth $11 billion. If you buy the company with $10 billion in cash and wait 5 years to sell it, you will make $1 billion from the sale at $11 billion and $2.5 billion from the cash. A total of a 25% return over 5 years.

If you did the same transaction as an LBO and used $9 billion of debt out of the $10 billion purchase price you would make a much higher return. Over the 5-year holding period you could pay down $2.5 billion of debt with the cash generated from the company. Then when you sell for $11 billion you would only have to pay back $6.5 billion of debt. Your total proceeds would be:

$11 billion sale - $6.5 billion of debt = $4.5 billion.

And on top of that you only invested $1 billion of your own money, so your total return is 350%.

Private equity firms usually try to do this with companies that generate a lot of cash to pay down the debt and have low price to earnings (P/E) multiples. We will go over P/E multiples in the next chapter.

The next 11% of Harvard's portfolio is natural resources which does not apply to us and includes hard assets, timberland, mining, and other land that provides natural resources.

The next 12% is real estate. Within real estate investing there is an entire industry breakdown similar to the equity investing industry we talked about. Many people choose to invest in real estate as rental properties or other forms of real estate either instead of investing in stocks or as a part of their portfolio. The benefits to real estate investing vs. stock market investing can include monthly reliable rental income, tax breaks, less risk, and a generally greater ability to use debt in transactions. Flipping a house is very similar to the LBO that we talked about earlier where you can use the cash from the investment to pay down the debt and make very large returns. The downside to personal real estate investing is that it takes a lot more effort than stocks to purchase and maintain a property as well as deal with tenants. At any time, a pipe could break that you are on the hook for, you have to pay a 5% to 10% transaction fee on every purchase, and you can't just sell it whenever you want because real estate is not a liquid asset.

Let's put ourselves in the shoes of the landlord from our Korean apartment example. The total value of the apartment was $200k and the rent from our example was $12k per year. In this case, the landlord is making 6% of the total investment every year plus he has the ability to sell the apartment in the future for more and can use debt to make his returns larger. This assumes that the apartment is never vacant and nothing else goes wrong.

Alternatively, the landlord in Korea could invest in a Real Estate Investment Trust (REIT). A REIT is a real estate stock market instrument available to anyone. A REIT gives you the returns of a large pool of real estate investments. At the time of this writing, one of the largest REITs is aptly named $REET and currently has a 6% dividend. This means that by owning this stock they pay you 6% of the value of your investment every year as a dividend. In this case, the landlord could save a lot of time and effort by investing in a REIT instead of buying his own real estate. In either case, REITs and real estate investments that generate less than market average returns should not be a part of our portfolio because we are trying to beat market averages.

After real estate in Harvard's portfolio comes fixed income. Fixed income mainly includes bonds which investment managers also invest in. Investment managers invest in bonds to help limit their downside risk. Bonds are agreements by the government or a corporation to pay you a fixed return on your investment each year. We can write a whole book on bonds as the bond market is actually larger than the stock market, but that book would be called "7 Years to Break Even" as the current 30-year treasury bond pays out a total of 1.5% per year, less than expected inflation. Bonds are generally compared by their yields which is how much per year they pay investors. The main thing to remember about bonds is that when their yields go down the stock market goes up since investment managers must put more money into stocks to achieve their 5% to 15% returns.

People usually say that investing in government bonds is without risk because you can only lose money if the United States fails and defaults on its debt. This could never happen unless the USA lost a war or no longer existed. Treasury bonds are at the core of so many essential systems to society that they could never be defaulted on while the government is still running. This is not much riskier than the S&P 500, for the stock market to never reach its current level again the United States would also have to fail. In fact, if the United States lost a war the corporations would still be worth more than the government bonds it promised to pay. Therefore, while not as consistent, the S&P may be less risky than government bonds while offering 5x to 10x the returns.

There are also corporate bonds which are the same as government bonds except they are guaranteed by a corporation. These are higher paying as there is a greater chance of a corporation defaulting than the US government. Both corporate and government bonds serve no place in our portfolio in the 7 Trades to a $1,000,000 strategy as they usually fall below the market averages.

In addition to bonds and REITs as instruments that provide income each year there are dividend paying stocks. A dividend is a payment you get from owning a stock. You have to hold for a certain period of time before you get the dividend but they are usually paid quarterly. Many growth stocks such as Microsoft and Apple provide very small dividends but when we talk about dividend paying stocks, we mean companies that are focused on paying and increasing their dividends. An example of this is Coca-Cola, a stock focused on its dividend and praised by Warren Buffet. From 1998 to today Coke's stock price has gone from $42 per share to $49 per share. During that time, it has paid an average dividend of about 3.5% per year. While there are some high paying dividend stocks, it is usually hard for a stock to pay a dividend when it is in its growth stage since they will be spending all their money on growth. Since we will be targeting growth stocks, we will not focus much on dividend paying stocks either.

After dividend paying stocks, the last category of safe investments include indexes. We have mentioned indexes already as they are a good barometer of the overall market. The three main indexes include the S&P 500, the NASDAQ, and the Dow Jones Industrial Average. You can invest directly in these indexes by using the ticker $SPY for the S&P, $QQQ for the NASDAQ, and $DIA for the Dow. The news usually focuses on the Dow, but all three indexes move very similarly. The indexes capture all the largest companies in the United States and underperformers are kicked out and replaced with new up and coming companies.

Investing in an index is like investing in the entire stock market. This is a very safe way to invest but you can make much more money in individual stocks. For example, in 2007, both Netflix and Blockbuster were in the S&P 500. If you took the average of them, you would still make money but you would do better to only invest in Netflix. The same is true today, the indexes hold a lot of dying and stagnant companies that we do not want to invest in so we will generally steer clear of investing in indexes when looking for growth.

Beyond the total market indexes there are indexes for almost every industry which can also affect our total returns. For example, at the beginning of the COVID Pandemic, let's say we wanted to short the entire airline industry because we knew travel would be at an all-time low. We could short the index $JETS because they hold many airlines and companies that manufacture planes. You could make a lot of money doing this but some of the companies in $JETS that manufacture planes also make car engines and some of the airlines in $JETS only focus on domestic travel which will be hit less than international. If you took your thesis one step further and researched which airline is most focused on international travel and shorted that stock, you would make a lot more money than simply shorting the airline index. In the next section we will talk about how to do this individual stock research.

The indexes that we are talking about are all structured as ETFs or exchange traded funds. ETFs are designed to create returns based on a certain group of stocks. The indexes we have mentioned so far all match their group exactly. If the S&P 500 goes up 10% then its ticker, $SPY will go up 10%. It is largely kept a secret that there are ETFs that are structured to go up more than the stocks they are based on. In 2019 the S&P 500 went up about 28%, if you had invested $100 in $SPY you would end the year with $128, a pretty solid gain but not getting us close to 7 trades to $1,000,000.

What is hidden from regular investors is that there are triple leveraged ETFs. Triple leveraged ETFs mirror the returns of a group of stocks multiplied by 3. In 2019, when $SPY went up 28%, $SPXL, the triple leveraged S&P index went up 84%. Eighty four percent gains on the S&P 500! I absolutely cannot understand why this is a secret. Anybody can invest in the triple leveraged S&P 500 which is considered the safest group of stocks in the world and almost double their money in a given year, just search for $SPXL on your broker platform. The same goes for the NASDAQ which has a triple leveraged ETF with ticker $TQQQ. The Nasdaq had a better 2019 than the S&P and $TQQQ went up 144%. One hundred forty four percent by investing in the NASDAQ! If you are going to buy ETFs, you should just buy the triple levered ones and triple your money. Look at the chart of the S&P again below.

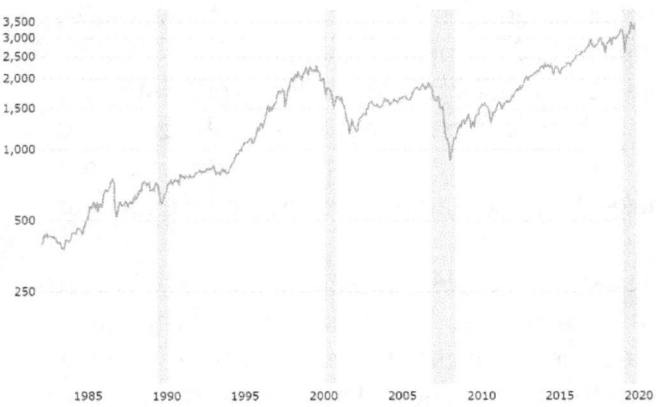

You may notice that it always goes up. The only way to lose money investing in the S&P is if the day you invest is the absolute peak of the United States economy for the rest of your life. That has never happened for anybody with a life spanning longer than 6 or 8 years and due to how important the stock market is today; 6 to 8 years will likely not happen again.

The one thing to be careful about with triple leveraged ETFs is that they also go down faster than the regular ETFs and it takes them longer to go back up. This is because they only mirror the percentages of the indexes. If something goes down 50% it needs to then go up 100% to get you back to where you started. If the S&P went down 16% it would only need to go up about 20% to get back to even. The triple leveraged ETF would be down 50% when the S&P is down 16% since it triples the returns. The triple leveraged ETF would only go back up 60% when the S&P is up 20% instead of the 100% it would need to get back to even. Due to this math, it is possible to lose more money in triple leveraged ETFs in a recession, but we are trying to focus on how to make the most money, not how to lose the least.

The fact that triple leveraged ETFs are hidden from public knowledge further proves that the financial world tries to profit on the ignorance of the masses. Everything you need to know about the world of finance is described in this chapter and it is pretty obvious that we should be focusing on how to achieve hedge fund returns ourselves instead of giving our money to investment managers.

In addition to triple leveraged ETFs, having a basic understanding of the institutional investment industry including hedge funds, investment management, private equity, and real estate investing is really all we need to begin investing in stocks. Contrary to popular belief, the whole investment industry is quite simple and that is probably why it is a secret.

Chapter 4:
Stocks and Why They Only Go Up

Now that we have explored The Bell Curve, why we should invest, and what the secrets of the investing industry are; we can finally talk about stocks. The number one thing to know about stocks is that they go up. This is why monkeys were able to beat the hedge fund managers and why the average annual index returns over the last 100+ years is 8.4%. If you pick any random stock for any random reason whether you are right or wrong, there is a good chance that the stock will go up. Our goal is not just to find a stock that will go up, it is to find a stock that will go up more than all the other stocks.

We are only going to cover factors that make stocks go up because I do not advocate for shorting stocks under any circumstances. When you buy a stock, you should have a reason for thinking it will go up more than other stocks. If you are right, you will make money, if you are wrong and the stock goes up the same as other stocks, you still make money. When you short a stock, you cannot make money from being wrong because if you are wrong, you lose money when the stock goes up. By shorting stocks, you are swimming against the tide. As we have shown, stocks usually go up consistently so shorting stocks lowers your chance of being correct and puts you on the wrong side of the randomness equation. The average gain of any stock chosen randomly is about 8%, to make the same amount of money shorting a stock you must find a stock that will be negative 16% from the averages to go 8% in the opposite direction. We want all the tailwinds that cause markets to go up to be on our side, not against us.

When you short a stock, you are borrowing the stock and promising to give it back at the same price later. In the meantime, you are selling the stock and hoping to buy it back later to return it. For example, if you borrow 10 shares of Margaritaville at $100 and sell them you will have $1,000 but still owe 10 shares of Margaritaville to the lender. If Margaritaville goes to $50 you can buy 10 shares back for $500 and return the 10 shares you owe. In this case, you make $500. In the case that Margaritaville goes up to $150 you must buy back the 10 shares for $1,500 to return them and you lose $500.

People get burned shorting stocks because you are putting yourself on the wrong side of the asymmetric risk equation. If Margaritaville goes to $1 per share you were as right as possible, but you only made $990 when you returned the 10 shares that you sold for $1,000. If Margaritaville goes to $500 per share, you will lose $4,000 when you return the shares. Four times more loss than the maximum amount of money you could have made.

On top of that you are betting against many forces that are not only trying to make the individual stock go up but make the entire market go up as a whole. These forces include the government, investors, billionaires, and people at the company working every day to make their stock go up. As we have proven in this book, most stocks go up, even monkeys can pick stocks that go up, so don't lose money hoping that stocks go down. Many short sellers complain that it is unfair that so many institutions continue to push stocks higher.

Shorting stocks and complaining that it is rigged is the same as going to a casino with the intention to double your money on a single roulette spin. You see a guy walking out with suitcases of cash and he tells you that the roulette wheel has been coming up black all night. You walk inside and the guy holding the door tells you that the roulette wheel is rigged for black, so you go over to the roulette wheel to check it out. You cannot get in because there's too many people crowded around the table, they are all betting black and winning every single time. You finally get a spot and the dealer whispers to you,

"Hey, I don't know if you know this, but this board is rigged for black"

You take all the money you came with and put it on red. Everyone looks at you confused, and the result is black again.

You lose all your money and yell,

"THIS GAME IS RIGGED!"

Yes, the game is rigged. Stocks have always gone up and they will keep going up. It is best to try to make money from this instead of betting against it.

So how do you determine which stocks will go up more than the general market does in a given year? The best way to do this is to think about the companies you interact with in your everyday life. No matter who you are, you interact with hundreds of companies directly every week and possibly every publicly traded company indirectly through Bacon's Law.

The six degrees of Kevin Bacon, also known as Bacon's Law, proved that over 99% of actors with listings on IMDB were within 6 degrees of being in a production with Kevin Bacon. For example, Warren Buffet made a cameo in "Entourage: The Movie". Billy Bob Thorton was also in Entourage and he was in "Jayne Mansfield's Car" which Kevin Bacon was in. Therefore, Buffet is only two degrees separated from Kevin Bacon.

We all have networks like this in our daily lives and we will hear about the products and companies that we should invest in far before Wall Street does if we are paying attention. The farther removed from a product you are, the more you should pay attention when you hear about it. For example, if you are an only child in college and your mom mentions that her friends are trying to buy sold out Crocs for their middle schoolers your ears should perk up. You are three degrees removed from the target market.

You→ your mom→ your mom's friends→ their middle schoolers

Word about the product still made its way to you, Crocs would be worth taking a look at. The stock ended up going up 500% during a stretch in 2020.

An obvious instance of a potential investment you interacted with is Zoom. If you were a college student during the COVID outbreak you were likely sent home from school in the middle of March. When online classes started again in the first week of April, it was the first time many Americans heard about Zoom. Even if you got all your news from Instagram meme pages you would still see everyone talking about logging into Zoom every day. You probably knew that people at other colleges were using Zoom and it would not be hard to find out that businesses were using Zoom too. The first week of April when most people logged onto Zoom for the first time the stock was trading at $100 per share. In the next 6 months it would go up to over $500 per share. This is enough of a gain to make millions of dollars with a very small investment using the options strategies we will talk about next chapter. If you were paying attention to the stock market and looking for your next trade, you would not have missed out on Zoom.

To break down the Zoom investment into a formula that we can replicate we can say that we had a thesis and a catalyst. This is broken down below:

Thesis: Zoom will add more users than expected.
Catalyst: The COVID Pandemic leading to remote learning and working.

The most important thing about our thesis is that its result is something more than what is expected by the broader market. If the market had already expected Zoom to add as many users as it did the stock would have already been trading at $500 per share.

Efficient market theory states that every single known possibility is already included in a stock price. This means that all information and possibilities have been evaluated by individual investors who have bought or sold the stock to the level that it currently sits. To make money our thesis has to beat expectations. For example, let's say there is a Christmas Tree company that only sold Christmas trees and the stock was trading at $100 in July when no Christmas trees are sold. You could trick yourself into investing in this company with the following formula.

Thesis: This company will sell more Christmas Trees in the winter months.
Catalyst: People buy more Christmas trees during Christmas.

You would be wrong here because you did not include in your thesis that the company will sell more Christmas trees *than expected*. Your original thesis has nothing to do with market expectations. The market obviously expects the Christmas tree company to sell more trees during Christmas otherwise the company would be worthless since they are selling none in July. You have to structure your investment thesis based on something that will happen beyond the market expectations.

When choosing your catalyst, you are looking for one or multiple reasons why the thesis will be true. The catalyst also must be a reason that is more important than expected. Every catalyst is already being considered by Wall Street, so we have to find the ones that matter.

You will never be able to come up with a catalyst that nobody else has thought about because everything is priced into a stock at a certain extent. Where the stock price currently sits is a combination of everyone's thoughts on the company evaluating every known catalyst. Stocks go up as the positive thesis is proven correct and go down as the negative thesis is proven correct.

Your very existence was priced in decades ago when the market was valuing Standard Oil's expected future earnings based on population growth that would lead to your birth, what age you would get a car, how many times you would drive your car every week, how many times you take the bus/train, etc. Anything you can think of has already been priced in, even the things you are not thinking of. Therefore, we must think about what will happen beyond expectations.

To understand the efficient market hypothesis, we can use the oversimplified example of a pharmaceutical company. Let's say Margaritapharma is developing a new drug that is awaiting approval. The market believes that there is a 50% chance the drug will be approved. If the drug is approved Margaritapharma will be worth $20 per share and if the drug is not approved, it will be worth $10 per share. The company would trade at exactly $15 per share. If you knew that the drug had a 100% chance of being approved, you would buy the stock because your thesis is that the drug has a greater chance of being approved *than expected*.

Thesis: The drug has a greater chance of being approved than expected.
Catalyst: Insider information that the drug will 100% be approved.

Reflecting further on Zoom, the stock went up from its pre-Pandemic levels by the first week of April but it continued to add users and grow revenue at a pace faster than the market expected. The stock continued to go up because it continued to beat the rising market expectations.

To determine if a catalyst will beat market expectations you have to have an idea of what the market expectations are. This information is readily available through sell-side analysts and the companies own forecasts. Sell-side analysts cover every stock individually and make forecasts for each quarter. While every company has different indicators of growth, the most important ones are revenue and earnings. Revenue is how much total money the company brings in from sales of their products or services. Earnings is how much money they keep after all their expenses. We will go into this in more detail at the end of the chapter. In the case of Zoom, when the pandemic broke out, many sell-side analysts upgraded their forecasts for Zoom. When sell-side analysts upgrade their forecasts the stock usually goes up that same day as the market begins to price in greater expectations for the company.

Sell-side analysts cover almost every stock and give buy, sell, or hold ratings on each one as well as a price target. In the news, you will often see headlines such as "Goldman Sachs upgrades Zoom price target to $600" or "JP Morgan downgrades Boeing to a Sell rating." Usually, the upgraded stock will benefit from these headlines and the downgraded stock will fall. When analysts talk about stocks, they will also use the terms "bullish" and "bearish". Bullish means you think the stock will go up and bearish means you think the stock will go down. The reason for these terms is that a bull uses its horns to attack up and a bear uses its claws to attack down.

Companies report their numbers once per quarter and can have wild moves on these days as we find out how the company is actually doing. If you looked at revenue expectations for Zoom in the first full quarter after the pandemic, you would see that they were already much higher than before the pandemic. Every analyst expected Zoom to have higher revenue but the revenue they announced was even higher than that expectation. Zoom continued to outperform during the pandemic and that is part of why the stock made a 500% move.

Knowing that a company will beat expectations is not always enough for the stock to go up. It must be a large enough factor in the company to affect its value. At the start of the Pandemic 3M was the largest mask maker in the world. We knew that the Pandemic would be a huge catalyst for mask sales so an investment thesis could look like this.

Thesis: 3M will sell more masks than expected.

Catalyst: The pandemic will force people to buy more masks than ever before.

Your thesis would be correct, but you would not make any money because mask sales would not cause 3M stock to go up. Masks are only .2% of 3M's total business so even if mask sales went up 1,000% it would barely cause a ripple in 3M's business. On top of that, even if you thought mask sales could go up 100,000% which is not outside the realm of possibility; 3M would not have the infrastructure to produce that many masks, so there is no situation where their revenue could be significantly affected by the demand for masks. 3M's stock consistently fell during the pandemic.

On the other hand, there is a company called Alpha Pro Tech $APT. They make 80% of their revenue from protective equipment including masks and hazmat suits. To them a 1,000% increase in demand for PPE would have a huge effect on their business. APT stock went from $3 before the Pandemic to a high of $41 at the start of lockdowns. More than a 1,000% gain.

The best way to know if your thesis will materially affect the company is to read their 10-K. A 10-K is a full report on a company that is filed once per year with the SEC. They are available to everyone and can be found on the company's investor website. Reading a 10-K is the best way to understand a company. 10-K's list out the company's entire business model, all positive catalysts that they are considering, all risk factors that they are considering, and their actual numbers.

You do not have to read the whole 10-K as they can be over 100 pages but the more you read the more you will be able to determine which parts are important and which parts you can skip. To successfully find companies to invest in, you must be aware of your surroundings and look for opportunities in your life and on whatever investing platforms you read. Then determine if that stock has a thesis and catalyst that make sense through reading the 10-K and researching the industry.

The methods for picking stocks that we have discussed so far are all fundamental reasons for the stock to go up. This means that we think the company will become more valuable based on growth within the company.

Another theory of investing is called technical investing. Technical investing is based on looking at charts and finding patterns. Some technical investors prefer to look at the charts without even knowing the name of the company so that they remain unbiased.

While many people swear by the charts, there has never been a study that shows any of these patterns work in predicting the movement of a stock. In fact, a simulation ran on all S&P stocks over a 5-year period that bought when one of the technical buy indicators appeared and shorted when one of the sell indicators appeared found that using technical analysis had worse returns than the indexes. While there is a whole industry of technical investing, it is human nature to look for patterns in random data. When randomly generated charts are given to technical investors, they cannot tell the difference from real stock charts.

Beyond fundamental and technical reasons to buy a stock, many people purchase equities for speculative reasons. It is an old adage to compare investing in the stock market to betting on the winner of a beauty pageant. If you were betting on the winner of the beauty pageant, evaluating the contestants would certainly be a factor. The largest factor would be evaluating who the judges think the winner should be. In investing, you can't make money if the greater market never catches on and agrees with your thesis. John Maynard Keynes famously said that "the market can remain irrational longer than you can remain solvent". This means that you can eventually run out of money before you are proven right. Part of deciding to make an investment is deciding if the market will eventually catch on to your way of thinking. When you invest in speculative stocks, you are hoping that the market does not catch on to your way of thinking which is why we should usually stay away from them.

There have been many stock market bubbles throughout history. Famous ones include the Tulip craze, the dot-com bubble, the '08 housing market, and in recent years cryptocurrency and weed stocks. In all these cases the value was being driven by pure speculation instead of fundamental reasons. While there is a good amount of speculation in Zoom, the company continued to beat revenue and user expectations throughout the Pandemic and is set up to be one of the greatest beneficiaries of a continued shift to remote working and learning. Compare this to Tilray, a cannabis company with no history of beating expectations and no large-scale distribution plan that went from $20 per share to $300 per share in one month during the cannabis craze of September 2018. Tilray only had a handful of employees at the time. Investing in Zoom is a bet that the company will continue to grow and beat market expectations. Investing in Tilray was a bet that somebody else would pay more than you before the market returned to rationality.

Investing in speculative stocks like Tilray invokes the greater fool theory. This is a theory in investing that there is a greater fool than you who will eventually pay more for your bad investment. In the case of Tilray, the stock went down to $5 per share just two years after hitting $300 and you can only wonder when the people who bought it at the top ended up selling. There are enough good companies with fundamental growth stories for us to invest in that we can avoid investing in speculative stocks.

While speculative stocks move the most, you will find that some stocks like Coca-Cola never move at all. You can have the best catalyst and thesis in the world for Coke and it likely would not make you very much money because the stock barely moves. The most important thing to look at when determining how high a stock can go is its Market Capitalization or Market Cap. Market Cap is the total value of the company to the stock market. It is calculated by multiplying the stock price by all the shares outstanding. You don't have to do this calculation yourself because a stock's Market Cap is always listed on whatever investing platform you use. The confusing thing about Market Cap is that each stock has a different number of shares outstanding and many beginning investors confuse stock price with market cap or total company value. For example, Apple is the most valuable company in the world with a Market Cap above $2 trillion. Netflix is certainly a large company but only 10% as large as Apple with a Market Cap at around $200 billion. Netflix stock trades at $500 per share and Apple trades at $100 per share even though Apple is 10 times larger than Netflix. While this is counterintuitive, you must ignore the share price when thinking about how high a stock can go up.

For example, if Margaritaville was worth $100 million and had 1 million shares outstanding, the stock would cost $100 per share. If they had 100 million shares outstanding the stock would cost $1 per share. The amount of shares outstanding is almost completely random and is determined in the infancy of a company and grown over time. We do not care at all about the amount of shares outstanding because it has nothing to do with the value of the company. Therefore, we do not care at all about the stock price. If Margaritaville split its stock, which companies often do, to 1 billion shares and each share only cost 10 cents it would not make any difference on how the stock moves or our investment analysis.

This is a very important concept and is the easiest way to tell if an investor knows what they are doing.

A beginning investor might think that it is easier for them to double their money on Apple stock starting at $100 per share because it only has to go up $100 per share to double. Comparing this to Netflix, the $500 Netflix has to go up $500 per share to double. In reality, for Netflix to double, the Market Cap has to go up by $200 billion and for Apple to double the Market Cap has to go up by $2 trillion. Even if Apple acquired Amazon (a $1.6 trillion dollar company) and Netflix for free it still would not be worth $4 trillion. It is much easier for Netflix to go up in value than

Apple even though the stock price is higher because Netflix has a smaller market cap.

When investing in companies, a company with a lower market cap has higher upside since there is more room to grow. Do not get tricked into thinking stocks with low stock prices have more room to grow because the stock price has nothing to do with the market cap.

The simplest way to think about this is to consider two government defense companies, let's call them Margarita Defense and Lockheed Margarita, both are going to get $1 billion dollar contracts from the government to produce weapons. Margarita Defense's stock price is $10 per share and their Market Cap is $10 billion dollars. Lockheed Margarita's stock price is $100 per share and their Market Cap is $1 billion dollars. Which company would you invest in?

The correct answer is Lockheed Margarita because a $1 billion dollar increase in value would double the value of the Lockheed Margarita and drive the stock from $100 to $200 per share because it was only worth $1 billion before. Margarita Defense will go to $11 per share since a $1 billion dollar increase is equal to a 10% gain when the company was already worth $10 billion. It is extremely important to understand that stock price has nothing to do with the value of the Margarita Defense, and that to judge the value of a company you have to look at the Market Cap.

We saw this example earlier with our mask making company Alpha Pro Tech $APT. At the beginning of the Pandemic, APT's stock price was at $3 but more importantly their Market Cap was only $40 million. To double your investment on APT the company would only have to gain $40 million in value. If Apple gained $40 million in value your investment would only go up by .002%.

After Market Cap, you should look at a stock's volume to see if it will move. Volume becomes more important when we start trading options, but it is something that we should still consider. Volume is the number of times per day that a stock is bought and sold. Apple is bought and sold about 100 million times per trading day. This means that efficient market theory is working most effectively on Apple. With 100 million trades per day every catalyst and possibility is certainly being evaluated by somebody.

On the other hand, a stock like Callaway ($ELY), a leading manufacturer of golf equipment and apparel, has a low volume. If you had the following investment thesis you may be right, but the low volume would hurt your returns.

Thesis: Increased golf activity will cause Callaway to sell more golf equipment than expected.

Catalyst: People picking up golf and playing more because it is a Pandemic friendly sport.

Unfortunately, Callaway only has a volume of 500k trades per day and is not a stock that typically moves at all. The best way to play this would be to buy right before the earnings announcement since the market is generally not paying attention to Callaway. More on earnings plays later.

Another way to see how a stock moves is by looking at its Beta Coefficient. Each stock has a Beta Coefficient that represents how it moves against the overall market. The Beta represents the volatility of the stock compared to the overall market.

If a stock has a Beta of 1 that means it is strongly correlated to the moves in the general market. If a stock has a Beta of more than 1 than that means that the stock is more volatile than the market and will move more than an average stock, most stocks that we are trading will fit into this category. High beta stocks go up more when the market is up and down more when the market is down. Stocks we should avoid have Betas less than 1 because that means they barely move. Coca-Cola has a Beta of .56 and is our example of a stock that does not move. Apple has typically gone up faster than the market and has a beta of around 1.3. You can find a stock's beta coefficient usually listed on your broker website.

Beyond revenue and earnings there are a few other key performance indicators (KPIs) to understand about companies that can help you create an investment thesis. Each individual company has its own KPIs that Wall Street will look at when valuing the company. It is easy to find out these KPIs when you are researching the stock, reading analysis, and looking at the 10-K. For example, a stock like Netflix will report their total subscribers as a KPI. If Netflix revenue jumped but their subscribers did not, it is likely because they raised their prices. This would be a less important factor than if they gained more subscribers. Therefore, for a company like Netflix you could make a more compelling argument by using their main KPI of subscribers.

Thesis: Netflix will add more subscribers than expected.
Catalyst: People are staying at home during the pandemic which will force them to download Netflix.

Another example of a KPI that is different from revenue and earnings came right before Tesla made their parabolic run. In 2019 the main KPI for Tesla was production volume on the Model 3. While the company had enough demand for millions of Model 3s, they were not able to produce enough to meet the demand and short sellers believed they would run out of money before they ever did. The investment thesis below was used by the ambulance driver who famously made a 100,000% return by investing in Tesla around this time.

Thesis: Tesla will be able to produce more Model 3s than expected.
Catalyst: Elon Musk is currently sleeping on the floor of the factory and dedicating 23 hours a day to ramping up production on the Model 3.

When Tesla met production demands on the Model 3, the stock began an unprecedented run based on achieving that KPI. By understanding the KPIs of a company you can focus on what will make the company increase in value and you create more specific and informed investments.

After KPIs most companies report some measure of EBITDA. EBITDA is an acronym for earnings before interest, taxes, depreciation, and amortization. Interest and taxes are not factors we have to think about when choosing which stocks to invest in. Depreciation is basically an accounting theory that allows companies to pay less taxes by saying that their equipment losing value is an expense. Companies only have to pay taxes on their earnings so if they say their $100 million dollar factory lost 10% of its value then they can take $10 million off their earnings which lowers their taxes even though they did not actually lose anything. Depreciation is a real factor in businesses that require a large number of factories and equipment to produce goods since they have to continue to upkeep those factories. However, since we are mostly investing in technology stocks, we do not need to think about depreciation very much. Technology stocks do not make or sell anything that requires factories or depreciating equipment. The same goes for amortization which is similar to depreciation but with intangible assets and loans.

EBITDA is important because EBITDA and earnings are used often as the basis for multiples. To tell if a company is over or undervalued you can look at their multiples compared to similar companies in the same industry. A multiple is a valuation method that multiplies a KPI by a certain multiple to get the Market Cap. This method is used by the broader investment industry and works well for established companies that are not expected to grow very fast in the near future. For example, Wal-Mart has a price to earnings multiple of 22.7x. This means that their Market Cap is 22.7x the amount of money they earn in a year. Wal-Mart's Market Cap is around $440 billion. Target does essentially the same thing as Wal-Mart and their price to earnings ratio is 23.6x but their Market Cap is about $80 billion. This means that Wal-Mart and Target are valued at essentially the same multiple of their earnings. Wal-Mart earns about 4x more money than Target and is worth about 4x as much. Amazon, on the other hand, has a price to earnings multiple of 126x and a Market Cap of about $1.64 trillion. This means that Amazon's earnings are valued about 4x higher than Wal-Mart's because their multiple on earnings is 126x and this stems from a multitude of reasons. Amazon has a larger market share of a faster growing industry and is in many other industry verticals that have larger potential than Wal-Mart.

Using multiples only works with mature companies like Wal-Mart and Target and doesn't hold much weight in high growth tech stocks. If you are interested in investing in mature companies, such as Wal-Mart or Target, it is useful to look at their earnings multiples to determine if they are over or undervalued compared to their peers.

You can use revenue multiples, subscriber multiples, and other industry specific multiples as well but you have to always compare companies to their competitors. People usually run into mistakes by comparing multiples or metrics across industries. You could compare a revenue multiple between Uber and Lyft which both trade at about 3x revenue, this means that their market cap is 3x the revenue they generate. It would not make sense to compare a revenue multiple between the ride sharing companies and Zoom which trades at 100x revenue. If you saw that Uber was trading at 5x revenue and Lyft was trading at 2x revenue this means that the market is down on Lyft. If you think the market will start to believe Lyft revenue is just as valuable as Uber, then investing in Lyft has merit even if the company does not make more money. Lyft stock in this scenario can go up through multiple expansion if people were to value them similar to Uber.

You can go to business school and learn more about all of these concepts in depth but the outline above is enough for us to start investing and making money with options. The most important things to take away from this chapter are that stocks always go up and that we must beat market expectations to gain an edge. If you are able to look at KPIs and determine market expectations, there is nothing stopping you from beating the market. Even if you are wrong you still have a puncher's chance because monkeys did not know anything about stocks when they beat the most sophisticated investors.

Chapter 5:
Options

"Play the game for more than you can afford to lose, only then will you learn the game"

- Winston Churchill

Congratulations, you made it or skipped to the options chapter where I will teach you how you can make seven trades to a million with your pocket change. Most people will tell you to stay away from options because they are riskier than stocks. The main reason options are more risky than stocks is because they have an expiration date. If you invest in a stock and nothing happens you can always sell the stock. If you invest in an option and nothing happens that option could expire worthless depending on the option. However, while stocks usually go up, they can't go up 100,000%, options can.

Options are derivatives of stocks meaning that they are based on the underlying value of the stock itself. They are sold in contracts of 100 that allow you to either buy or sell the underlying stock at a certain price. Each option contract has a strike price where you can either buy or sell the stock depending on the kind of option. Each option contract also has a specific date when the option expires.

Options allow you to maximize your returns by allowing you to capture only the upside of the stock without having to pay for the entire stock itself. With stocks, let's say you have $1,000, it's January 1st and Margaritaville is trading at $100 per share. You think that the stock will go up $10 this month. You can buy 10 shares of Margaritaville and make 10% from your $1,000 and get a $100 gain.

This is considered a good investment, but 10% gains will not get you to a million in 7 trades.

With options you can pay for the right to buy the stock for $100 on February 1st when you think the stock will be worth $110. Let's say that the value of that option is $1 on January 1st when the stock is still at $100. You would be paying $1 for the right to buy the stock at $100 on February 1st. So, you buy 1,000 options for $1,000 at $1 each. On February 1st if the stock goes to $110 you will have the right to buy 1,000 shares at $100 per share. This option would be worth $10 each because you could buy each share for $100 and then immediately sell them on the open market for $110. Instead of buying the 1,000 shares that you have the right to buy, you could sell that option for $10 each on February 1st. The 1,000 options you bought for $1 each you sold for $10 each and you turned $1,000 into $10,000 in one month even though the stock still only went up 10%.

This is how we can easily make huge amounts on our investment without putting a lot of money upfront. To make $10,000 through buying Margaritaville stock in January you would have had to invest $100,000. With options you can make the same return on the same stock with only $1,000. The difference is you can also lose it much easier.

If we take the same example and assume you are wrong about your thesis. Instead of Margaritaville going up to $110 per share on February 1st the stock stays at $100 per share. Your options still give you the right to purchase 1,000 shares of Margaritaville at $100 per share, however, anybody can buy 1,000 shares for $100 on the open market. Your option is worthless and would be worth $0 on its expiration date. In this case you would lose $1,000 or 100% and if you had bought the stock instead you would have lost nothing.

Options notation includes the strike price which is the price you have the right to buy the stock at, in this case $100. The option will also include the expiration date which is the date you have the right to either buy or sell the stock. If you buy a call option, that gives you the right to buy the stock. A put option gives you the right to sell the stock. The option from our example above was a call option and would be written like this. $100 2/1 Call, $100 is the strike price, 2/1 is the date, and call means we have the right to buy.

Puts work the same way but in the opposite direction. If you bought the $100 2/1 Put option, you would have the right to sell shares at $100 on February 1st to the option writer. If the stock went to $90 per share this option would be worth $10 each because somebody could simply buy the stock on the open market for $90 and sell it to the option writer for $100. The option writer is the entity selling you the option. In most cases this is an algorithm run by a bank or other large financial institution. Similar to what we talked about with stocks, I recommend only focusing on call options because stocks usually go up.

In the examples above we purchased strike prices at the price the stock was currently trading, these are called "at the money" options or ATM options. We could also buy options that are "in the money" or ITM, which means they are below the price the stock is trading. If Margaritaville was trading at $100 and we bought the $90 2/1 Calls, they would cost around $10 per option since the stock is trading at $100. If the stock went up to $110, the option would be worth $20 since we have the right to buy it at $90. Since we paid $10 for this option in this case you would make 100% on your investment instead of the 1,000% you could make with at the money (ATM) options. The main difference here is that if the stock stays at $100 per share you don't lose your money, the option would still be worth $10 per option because the strike is at $90. When you buy a stock in the money you will not lose the entire investment if the stock stays the same or goes down a bit because you are giving yourself some room. At the money options offer higher returns but higher risk.

In the money options are a less risky way to boost your returns. You will have lower returns, but you will be less at risk to lose the entire investment. On the other end of the spectrum, you can buy "out of the money" (OTM) options, which are options above where the stock is trading. If we wanted to buy $105 2/1 Calls these would be considered out of the money since they are above the current share price of $100. These would be much cheaper than ATM or ITM options since it is less valuable to be able to buy a stock above its current market value. Let's say that the $105 2/1 Calls cost only $.10 each and the stock still goes to $110 by our expiration date. In this case, since our strike price is $105 our options are worth $5 each. Since we bought them for $.10, we had a 5,000% percent return. If we spent $1,000 buying the $105 2/1 Calls for $.10 each and sold them for $5.00 each, we would have $50,000 after the trade. Using OTM options is the way that people make insane returns in short amounts of time in the market.

When picking a stock to buy options on, you must pay very close attention to volume. Since we do not plan on exercising the option and buying all the shares, we will have the right to buy we need somebody to sell the option to. On obscure stocks and stocks that have low volume, it is possible that you can get stuck with no buyers for your option. It is also possible that you will have to sell the option for much less than it should be worth because there are limited buyers. I only recommend trading options on stocks with decent volume so that you do not get stuck with options that you can't sell.

In reality, options are not quite as easy as the examples above because you still have to beat market expectations. If many people thought that Margaritaville would be worth $110 on February 1st then the at the money options when the stock is at $100 would already cost close to $10 per contract. Option prices vary depending on market expectations for the stock and the amount of time until the expiration date. Options that have further expirations in the future are more expensive because there is more time for the stock to go up. If in January, we purchased calls that expired in December instead of February they would be much more expensive because there is a higher chance that the stock would go up 10% in a year than in a month. On the other hand, options that expire soon are cheaper because there is less of an expectation for the stock to move as much. If on January 1st we bought $110 1/2 Calls which expect the stock to go up 10% in one day, they could be worth as little as $.01 each. If something were announced that sent the stock to $120 on that day your option would have gone up 10,000% in a day since they would be worth $10 per contract.

Since you can sell your options any time before the expiration date the price of an option fluctuates similar to a stock. If the market believes the stock has a higher chance to go up, the options will become more expensive and vice versa. To use the most binary example of a pharmaceutical company, let's say that the market already knows the company has a drug with a 50% chance to be approved. The stock price would have priced in the value of the drug and the probability of the drug being approved. If the company announces the exact day that we will discover if the drug is approved or not, the stock price may not fluctuate much because this is already priced in. However, the options expiring after the announcement will get much more expensive because the chance of the stock going up by that time just rose.

For this reason, options are more expensive near obvious catalysts. Options expiring the day after an earnings call will be much more expensive than the day before.

Stocks like Coca-Cola that barely move will have very cheap options. ATM options on $KO for one month out could be worth around $.50. While a speculative stock like Tesla could see ATM options of over $100 per contract in the same time frame. This is because market expectations are for Coke to barely move and for Tesla to move wildly. Understanding how options move is completely different to understanding how stocks move and the best way to learn is by doing. Even if you fully understand how options pricing works the best way to get familiar with how they move is buying them. When you own an option, you can follow it easily and see how it moves with the underlying stock and as it gets closer to expiration.

While trading options you will naturally get a sense for how they move, option movement is also quantified in formulas called "The Greeks".

Delta

Delta is the most important Greek because it most easily quantifies how your option will move with the underlying stock. Delta is simply the amount of money your contract will move in accordance with every dollar the underlying moves. In other words, if our options on Margaritaville for $1 had a .3 delta. and the price of the Margaritaville moves up $1 to $101, the option is now worth $1.30 since we add the .3 delta to the option price. Conversely, if the underlying stock moves down $1, the option is worth $.70. This is a simplistic way of looking at it, as other things can affect delta such as fundamentals and volatility, but that is what delta means.

Delta is affected most by how close the strike price is to the current price of the underlying stock. Farther OTM options have less Delta, farther ITM options have more, and ATM is typically around .5. Knowing delta is important in measuring risk/reward because it will tell you how much the value of the option will move for or against you as the underlying stock moves.

Gamma

If Delta is the speed in which the price moves, gamma is the acceleration or rate of change of the delta. Gamma only affects how the Delta changes with the underlying stock. What Gamma measures is how much Delta changes after each subsequent dollar change. Here is an example to illustrate:

> Buy call option XYZ $100 with .3 delta and .01 gamma for $1.00

> Price of the underlying stock moves up $1

> Call is worth $1.30 since the delta was $.30, the new delta value is now .40 meaning that if the stock goes up another dollar the option price will go up by 40 cents. This is because the delta changed from .3 to .4 as the stock went up $1 since the gamma was .1.

The example is again a simplistic way of looking at it, but don't miss the point, Gamma will accelerate the price change in your option as the underlying changes and is an important factor in determining risk/reward.

Unlike Delta, Gamma is heavily affected by the expiration date, and Gamma increases as you get closer to expiry, and is much smaller the farther out you buy. It is not affected heavily by how ITM or

OTM the option is (although there is a slight increase the closer you get to ATM).

Gamma is a derivative of Delta which is a derivative of the option price which is a derivative of the stock price. A beginner does not have to focus on the Gamma but sometimes it is interesting to check and see how we can expect the Delta to change.

Theta

Think of Theta as the amount of money you have to spend per day to hold the contract, or the amount you get paid per day to sell one. I like to think of Theta as how much money I will lose per day if the underlying stock trades sideways or stays the same.

Theta is increased as you get closer to your expiry date. At about 30 days to expiration, Theta begins to accelerate faster. ATM strikes tend to have the most theta, where ITM strikes have enough intrinsic value that they are not affected as much and OTM strikes go for less premium so there is less value to lose.

Theta is the main Greek that causes people to lose money with options. If you are close to expiration your Theta will be very high and could cause your option value to go down even if the underlying stock price goes up. Be careful when dealing with high theta.

For example, if we bought our $100 2/1 Calls on Margaritaville for $1 each and the stock stayed at $100, the option would slowly start to lose value. As we got within days of expiration the option would start to lose value faster since there is less time for the stock to go up. This would be expressed as rising Theta.

If the Theta is higher than the Delta that means that the option price will go down even if the stock goes up $1 since the delta adds to the value as the stock goes up but the theta always subtracts from the option value as each day passes.

Vega

Vega is the amount the underlying moves in response to a 1% change in implied volatility. This is the reason behind the term "IV crush." Vega is greater the farther out you purchase your option, and greater the closer it is to being ATM (while OTM options have a slightly higher Vega than ITM, it's not by much).

Implied Volatility rank takes the past 52 weeks of implied volatility for the ticker and tells you what percentile its current IV resides. However, Vega can play in your favor if volatility increases. This can be a shrewd play if you catch a ticker a couple weeks before earnings or a large event like a drug approval.

There are a lot of other Greeks as well that we should not pay much attention to but the Greeks above can give you a sense of how you expect an option to move.

Option Strategies

Now that we understand what options are and how they move let's talk about some strategies using options. There are an abundance of options strategies that involve selling options and opening option spreads. I do not recommend using these strategies but just so that you are aware of them they are laid out below.

Covered Call

A covered call is a strategy that you can only use if you own at least 100 shares of a stock. The strategy is to sell calls above the stock price and collect the premium. If the stock goes up to that price you will have to sell the shares at that price but get to keep the premium. For example, if you own 100 shares of Margaritaville trading at $100 each you could sell the $110 calls for $1 each. Since you own 100 shares you would get $100 dollars for this. If the stock does not make it to $110 by the strike price you keep the $100. If the stock does make it to $110 or above you have to sell the stock for $110 each but you still keep the $100 from selling the options. People use this strategy because you can't lose money on the option but you can miss out on the upside if the stock goes to $115 since you still have to sell it at $110.

Covered Put

This is the opposite of a covered call and consists of selling puts below the trading price of the stock. If you think the stock will not go down this is free money because you get to keep the premiums on the option. If the stock does go down, you have to buy at the put price which would be above where the stock goes down to. If you sold puts on Margaritaville at the $100 strike for $1 each and the stock went down to $90 you would have to give up your shares of Margaritaville for $90 each. However, if you did not own the stock already you would have to buy the stock at $100 each and then sell it at $90.

Iron Condor

An Iron Condor is a strategy that you can use if you think the stock will trade sideways. This consists of selling one OTM Put below the trading price and one OTM call above the trading price. If the stock does not hit either the high or low strike you get to keep the premiums from both. This is an interesting strategy to use when the market is expecting big news and you expect no news. To use our example of a pharmaceutical company, if you think that the FDA ruling will be delayed you can buy an iron condor and make money from the option premium prices which will be high since they are expecting a large move in either direction.

Straddle or Strangle

A straddle or strangle is the opposite of an Iron Condor and should be used when you know a stock will have a big move, but you don't want to decide which direction. This consists of buying both calls and puts and hoping that the direction you choose is right enough that it outweighs the loss of one leg of the strategy. For example, if you knew Margaritaville was going to finish the month at either $90 or $110 and the $100 options were trading at $1 each you could buy both calls and puts. One will turn to $10 each and one will go to $0 but you will still profit.

There are also call and put spreads which consist of buying and selling both calls and puts to hedge your bets. We do not need to focus much on hedging our bets when trying to achieve market beating returns.

All the strategies above still require an edge to be successful. It is not as easy as buying Iron Condors on Coca-Cola, since the premiums are so low that you will barely make money, and if it does move you will lose a lot. The same can be said for straddles on FDA announcements because the premiums will be so high that losing one direction will not be profitable. For example, if Margarita Labs was a pharmaceutical company with an FDA announcement coming up the ATM calls and puts could be $5 each instead of the $1 we have used in our examples. If one leg goes to $10 and the other leg goes to $0 you did not make any money since your loss cancels out your gain. While the options strategies above are important to know, the options strategies that will help us achieve our 7 trades to a million consist solely of buying call options on stocks when we have an edge. There are three ways to do this, LEAPS, Mid-Term, and OHPs.

LEAPS

LEAPS stands for long-term equity anticipation securities and is any option that expires over a year away from the current date. LEAPS are similar to owning the stock except based on their delta they can go up or down much faster than the stock itself. LEAPs are good for when you have a catalyst that will play out over a long period of time. For example, the shift to electric cars will take years to catch on. If you bought Tesla LEAPs for a 3-year period not knowing when it would make its run but assuming it would eventually then you would be very happy today. LEAPS offer the lowest risk reward of any option because it would take years for them to go to 0 and you can sell any time before that, unless you find a Tesla, however, they likely will not go up 1,000%.

Mid-Term

Mid-Term options are for the period shorter than LEAPs but longer than a few weeks. Mid-Term options have a few use cases and should probably be the most common form of option we look to play. Mid-Term options are great for catalysts that play out over a few weeks or runups to certain catalysts. The saying "buy the rumor, sell the news" means that you should buy stocks on a rumor that something positive will happen and sell right before the news. This works because as the market prices in positive possibilities the stock goes up. If the news does not exceed the expectations of the market you often see stocks fall even on positive news because of a large run-up. For example, WWE always seems to have a run-up before Wrestlemania as the market prices in the possibility of larger than ever subscriber numbers. Whether they beat the expected subscriber numbers or not, buying Mid-Term options and selling just before Wrestlemania could be a great play here.

Again, there are no obvious plays. If everyone knew that WWE would run up before Wrestlemania then you could not beat market expectations. The duality of this leads to an investing myth where a hedge fund manager is walking with a journalist. The journalist spots a $100 bill on the ground and goes to pick it up. The hedge fund manager says, "don't waste your time, if that was really a $100 bill it wouldn't be on the ground".

The most common news events are quarterly earnings reports which can also have large run-ups. Buying Mid-Term options for hyped companies a few weeks before their earnings as the market prices in a large earnings beat is also a great strategy. Mid-Term options give you the ability to capture the upside of a medium-term catalyst with a medium level of risk depending on your strike price.

OHPs

OHPs are O'Hare Plays. These are the highest risk reward options possible and how we can make hundreds of thousands of percent on a single play. Chicago is the options trading capital of the United States and many of the options we buy will be written in Chicago. O'Hare is the name of the Chicago airport and the term originates from Chicago options traders making very risky and short-term plays. The idea is that you put all of your money on a single options trade with a short-term catalyst like an earnings report, drug announcement, merger announcement, or something that happens in a day. You then go to the airport and wait for the results of your play. If you are successful and achieve 100x to 1,000x returns you call your family and go on a lavish vacation. If you lose all your money, then you buy a ticket to another city and start a completely new life.

On the internet these are sometimes also called FD's, but the explanation of FDs is too crude for an investing book.

If your catalyst is something that will happen in one day then the best way to maximize your returns is to buy options as close as you can to that day which expire soon after the catalyst. By buying options right before the catalyst you do not have to deal with Theta decay from holding the option before the catalyst. By having them expire soon after, you can get them for as cheap as possible since the chances of the stock moving are lower for shorter periods of time.

Understanding your catalyst is very important here. If you think that a company will beat earnings but expect the market to price this in, then you will want to buy Mid-Term options and play the runup to earnings. If you expect a company to surprise the market, then you will want to wait for the day before earnings and buy OHP options.

In general, you can buy LEAPs or Mid-Term options for any catalyst depending on how much risk you want but you should only make OHPs when the catalyst is something that will happen in a single event.

The most important thing to remember about options is that the closer the expiration and the further they are out of the money, the more risk/reward you can achieve. The further the expiration and the more in the money they are, the lower the risk/reward.

The most important thing about options is that you still need to have an edge. Options are the best way to make money when we know a stock will do better than expectations but there is somebody on the other side of every options trade that disagrees with you. If a monkey throwing darts can beat them, we can beat them too.

Options are inherently confusing, but anybody can learn them. After a first read of this chapter you still may not get them or fully understand how they move. I can promise you that everything you need to know about them is written here but the easiest way to learn is to dip your toe in.

You can explain to somebody who has never had a Margaritaville Cheeseburger exactly how they taste. You can teach them to the point where they can describe to somebody else how a Margaritaville Cheeseburger tastes. But until you try one you can't really know.

You won't ever fully understand options until you start trading them.

Chapter 7:
Portfolio Management

Now that we know all the different kinds of investments we will be making and have developed an understanding on how to make them, we can start talking about how to structure our portfolio. If we remember Harvard's portfolio, only a small portion of it was in the stock market. We will have our entire portfolio in the stock market as you cannot get rich buying government bonds. Anybody that tells you to invest in bonds is giving you bad advice unless you already have $100 million dollars and are looking to live off the $2 million a year you would get from government bonds.

Our entire portfolio will be focused on 5 categories:

1. Stocks that only go up
2. Triple leveraged ETFs
3. LEAPS
4. Mid-Term Options Plays
5. OHPs

Stocks that only go up

Stocks that only go up are the growing stocks that we all know, Apple, Amazon, Google, Facebook, Microsoft, etc. These are the tech stocks that are integral to daily life and will continue to go up for the next 10 years. These don't have to be tech stocks, but they have to be proven stocks that you could tell anybody you are invested in without them questioning your strategy. If you want, you can even add the Nasdaq or S&P 500 regular ETFs to this section. The point of buying stocks that only go up is so that we have a safe section of our portfolio that will go up 15% to 30% no matter what. This is the risk management section of our portfolio; most recommendations say that you should take this portion and invest it in bonds because those are the safest investments. In this book, we assume that the chances of the stock market never reaching an all-time high is the same as the government never paying back its bonds. Therefore, we will take the 15% to 30% gains from stocks and ETFs that only go up instead of the 1% or 2% gains from government bonds.

Triple leveraged ETFs

If you don't know what triple leveraged ETFs are go back to chapter 3 where we talk about them at the end. Triple leveraged ETFs are riskier than the stocks that only go up but will provide us 3x the returns. It is important to note that you should not buy options on triple leveraged ETFs because it does the same thing as buying options on the underlying index ETFs and there is less liquidity. Many beginning investors make this mistake, but you will actually increase your returns by buying options on the regular ETFs instead of the triple leveraged ones.

For example, if the S&P 500 index is trading at $100 per share an ATM call option expiring that week may cost $1 each. On the triple leveraged ETF that same option would cost $3 each since the market knows that the triple leveraged ETF will triple whatever the underlying ETF does. The difference is that you would have less liquidity on the triple leveraged ETFs so you would have lower potential gains and open yourself up to the possibility of selling at a lower price than you should have to.

The triple leveraged ETF section of our portfolio should mainly consist of $TQQQ and $SPXL and we will expect between 50% and 90% gains on these every year.

What we are doing by buying stocks that only go up and triple leveraged ETFs with a section of our portfolio is making sure that we don't go to 0 and lose all of our money. Between these two base sections of your portfolio, you can expect 40% to 60% returns every year without any effort or thought as long as the market goes up, which it usually does. These sections will not get you to a million dollars in 7 trades but they will allow you to use the rest of your portfolio to go all out and still have a lot of money left if you are wrong on all of your options plays. For example, if 50% of your portfolio is in stocks that only go up and triple leveraged ETFs you can lose 100% of every single option play and you would still end the year with around 75% of what you started with since the first two sections will grow. The key to this strategy is to stick with it.

Never sell the stocks or the triple leveraged ETFs otherwise you can go to 0.

It does not make sense to regularly trade the stock or ETF sections of our portfolio because our strategy here is not to time the market. Never sell these positions, just continue to add to them. You may be tempted to sell on a day where the stock goes up to buy back in on a day where it goes down but in reality, stocks and market indexes fluctuate day to day with no predictable patterns. If you invested $10,000 in the S&P 500 in 1980 it would be worth over $900,000 today. However, if you took out the highest returning 5 days from each year you would only have about $440,000. It is impossible to know when those big 5 days each year will come but we should make sure we have our money invested when they do. The only way to guarantee this is by holding and not trading your stocks and ETFs.

LEAPS

LEAPS are a very important part of our portfolio and are one step riskier than triple leveraged ETFs. In many ways buying a LEAP is similar to buying a triple leveraged ETF on a single stock. You should buy LEAPS on stocks that you think will go up a lot in the next year but don't have a specific catalyst. It is a perfectly fine strategy to buy LEAPS on the stocks that only go up, but this is the part of our portfolio that will make or break us and a chance to buy your favorite stocks that you feel most strongly about.

You should buy your LEAPS for two years in the future with a strike price above where the stock is now but below where you expect it to go. For example, if you are buying LEAPS on Margaritaville currently trading at $100 and expect it to be at least $150 by the end of two years you should buy options at a strike of $125. The reasoning behind this is that if you are right it allows the investment to get less risky as it matures. Once Margaritaville passes your strike price, the option price can no longer go to 0 if it expires and thus your LEAP goes from risky to not as risky. The option becomes in the money over time and becomes a de-risked investment. This is a way to lock in the gains of your investment. If you bought the $150 strike your option would be much more of a race against the clock since the option would not become in the money until the very end.

The LEAPS section of our portfolio should be monitored closely but not traded. Keep up to date with the stocks you have LEAPS on and listen to all their earnings calls. Do not sell because of the movement in the stock under any circumstances, don't sell if it goes down too much and don't sell if it goes up too much. Only sell the LEAP if your thesis is proven wrong, otherwise hold for at least a year. The 100,000% gain we talked about earlier was a LEAP, he didn't sell when he was down 20% because his thesis on Model 3 production was still true. Nor did he sell when he was up 50,000% because the thesis was also still true.

As an aside, it never makes sense to sell a LEAP to lock in your gains unless you are going to take the money out and spend it. Usually, you are selling a good idea that is being proven right in exchange for another idea. Keep your good ideas in your portfolio and let them grow. On the other hand, sell your bad ideas as soon as it is clear that they are wrong. For example, let's say you bought Airline LEAPS at the start of the pandemic assuming that air travel would get back to normal. If you start seeing company reports and research that you trust which states that business travel may never get back to where it was, and that regular travel could take 5 years to return to normal then it may be time to sell your LEAPS.

Lastly, while we do not talk about taxes very much in this book, it is very beneficial to hold LEAPs for more than one year. When you hold a LEAP for more than a year, it becomes a long-term capital gain and is taxed at a much lower rate than a typical option is. This will make a huge difference and is why you should not sell the LEAP unless your thesis is proven wrong.

Mid-Term Options

Mid-term options plays are plays for a single catalyst that will play out over a couple of months. As we covered earlier, these could be seasonal trends, earnings reports, mergers, upcoming announcements, or anything that the market will react to over a medium period. The most important thing about these plays is that you should not try to force them. Maybe you will only have 5 a year that you really believe in and that is fine, keep this section of your portfolio as cash in between plays. The worst thing you can do is make a bunch of money on an option play you are sure about and then lose it all on one that you aren't sure about. If you do this, you won't have any money left for the next really good one that comes up.

Mid-term options plays are going to be the main source of our gains. For these plays, we are aiming at 300% to 600% returns and this is the core of the 7 trades to a million section of our portfolio. You should use a similar strategy to LEAPS where you buy strike prices about halfway between where the stock is trading now and where you expect it to be at the end of your holding period.

The main difference between mid-term options and LEAPS is that you will want to trade these. Since the holding period is short you will be subject to fluctuations in the broader market. If during your holding period, you think that something is happening that will keep the broader market down then you will want to sell these immediately. On the other hand, if something is happening that will make the broader market go up you will want to buy mid-term options on the indexes or the stocks that only go up. To trade mid-term options effectively you have to be very in tune to what is happening with the individual stock and with the broader market, you must check the news every day.

Many traders make the mistake of overtrading. You should go into every week with a game plan and not deviate from that plan. You should have reasons why you are buying or selling each mid-term option play. These options are very similar to gambling and it can become addictive to buy and sell them, for this reason you should make sure you are sticking to your game plan and not trading "for fun".

OHPs

O'Hare plays are the options we will buy that expire within a few weeks or within the next few days. We want to buy these for catalysts that will play out in one instance and that we expect to surprise the market. If we are playing an earnings call with no run-up, we can buy an option the day before the call and sell the morning after. This strategy will maximize our returns on OHPs. If the broader market has been down for a few days on no news you may want to buy calls expiring the next day for 1% or 2% OTM strikes, you can easily double your money on plays like this with very little effort. Keep in mind that the broader investing community suggests it should take over 10 years to double your money while targeting 7% annual gains. This small high risk/reward section of our portfolio is what will separate us the most from typical investors.

Using these short term options, we can achieve percent gains in the thousands in one or two days meaning that these are the highest risk reward plays in our portfolio. Because of the risk here we don't ever want to hold for more than a few days. If your thesis is proven right, sell immediately while you are up. If a gain is good enough for you to screenshot and share, then it is good enough to sell right there. Conversely, if you are down 70% it is better to save what's left than lose it all.

This chapter assumes that you have about $10,000 to invest. If you have significantly less than $10k you should have your entire portfolio in options until you get to that level. Once you are at $10,000, it makes sense to employ some sort of portfolio management to make sure your risk reward profile is always where you want it to be. Below are three examples of portfolios broken into the five core investment strategies we have discussed.

Warren Buffet:
25% Stocks that only go up
25% Triple leveraged ETFs
20% LEAPS on stocks you like
15% Mid-Term options plays
5% OHPs

Jimmy Buffet:
20% Stocks that only go up
20% Triple leveraged ETFs
30% LEAPS on stocks you like
20% Mid-Term options plays
10% OHPs

YOLO:
10% Stocks that only go up
10% Triple leveraged ETFs
45% LEAPS on stocks you like
20% Mid-Term options plays
15% OHPs

The key to portfolio management is to try to keep your percentages the same as certain parts of your portfolio grow and shrink so that you maintain the same risk profile. As you make gains in the short-term options section of your portfolio you will want to reinvest them into the stocks, ETFs, and LEAPS that you have selected. The other key is to realize that you should always have a portion of your mid-term and OHP investments as cash on hand. You should always keep some level of cash and make sure that you are not overtrading in your options sections.

You should pick a portfolio breakdown that works for your goals and your current situation and stick with it. While it may feel counterintuitive to trim winning positions to reinvest in the safer parts of your portfolio, you should keep in mind that this is a way of locking in your gains. Any of the portfolios above can achieve 1,000s of percent gains while limiting downside so sticking with them will never be a bad decision. Unless you have around $10,000 invested, I recommend just trying to get there with the options plays you can afford.

Beyond just setting up a balanced portfolio that allows you to take risks and protect yourself from losing everything, there is also a benefit to diversification. Let's say the strongest thesis you have is that the United States online gambling market will grow faster than expected. You may be tempted to make the LEAPs portion of your portfolio consist of DraftKings, FanDuel, and Penn National Gaming. If you are correct all three will go up but if you are incorrect none of them will. You have chosen three different companies, but they all have the same thesis. This is the same as buying an index and you would do better to research which company is the best of the three and only invest in that one. When we diversify, we need a diversification of ideas not just a diversification of companies. If you are interested in two companies that are in the same industry just choose one. You will do better to invest in another idea represented by another company.

Now that we understand how the stock market works and how we can invest our money to make ridiculous gains, the question arises: what next? The answer is simple, get rich.

You have the knowledge to transform your pocket change into a vast wealth of insurmountable value. All it takes is focus and directing your analytic mind to current events while paying attention to publicly traded companies.

Emancipate yourself through these simple lessons of the stock market by using these methods for investing your money. I have shown you the path, but it is up to you to walk it.

You should center your whole attention on generating your wealth. Take hold of the reins of the market and ride the bull to a prosperous life of wealth and glory. The opportunity is truly infinite and there is no better time than now.

Your seven trades to a million are on this page but it is up to you to fill it out.

1)

2)

3)

4)

5)

6)

7)

www.ingramcontent.com/pod-product-compliance
Lightning Source LLC
Chambersburg PA
CBHW070649220526
45466CB00001B/355